Phillips

COLLECTORS GUIDES

CATS & DOGS

Text ©   Peter Johnson
Illustration ©   Phillips Fine Art
              Auctioneers
Edited by   Linda Doeser
Designed by   Strange Design Associates

Copyright © Dunestyle Publishing Ltd. and
Boxtree Ltd, 1988.

Boxtree Ltd.
36 Tavistock Street
London WC2 7PB

Conceived by Dunestyle Publishing Ltd.

ISBN 1 85283 232 0

Typesetting by Top Draw, London
Colour separation by J Film Process Co Ltd.,
Bangkok, Thailand
Printed in Italy by New Interlitho spa.

COLLECTORS GUIDES

CATS & DOGS

PETER JOHNSON

BOXTREE

Phillips, founded in 1796, has a reputation for specialisation. Its specialists handle fine art, antiques and collectors' items under more than 60 subject headings — a huge spectrum of art and artefacts that ranges from Old Masters and the finest antique furniture to cigarette cards and comparatively modern pop memorabilia. The auction group's Collectors' Centre, situated at Phillips West Two in Salem Road, Bayswater, London, is constantly recognising, defining and catering for new trends in collecting. It answers hundreds of queries a day from collectors, museums, dealers and the public at large. The shelves of its cataloguing halls are packed with a treasure-trove of objects, awaiting their turn to appear at auction. To varying extents, the scene there and in the main Mayfair salerooms (Phillips, 7 Blenheim Street, London W1Y 0AS; telephone 01-629 6602) is repeated at a score of Phillips branches elsewhere in Britain.

In a Phillips book about cats and dogs, it would not be out of place to pay tribute to Friend, the pet and companion of Harry Phillips, the founder of the firm. History records that Friend saved his master from drowning — and the event is commemorated in a number of antique collectables. Friend's story is told in Chapter 8.

Contents

Chapter One

Introduction

When King Edward VII died in 1910 a slender volume entitled *Where's Master?* was published under the name of his grief-stricken fox terrier, Caesar. It became a best-seller, as did a later book purporting to be the memoirs of Caesar's successor, George V's dog, Happy, which chronicled events relating to the new barking order within the royal walls. Both have become collectors' items today. There is a predicament of classification here for dealers: whether to place such outrageous gems of ephemera under 'royal collectables' or under the heading of 'pets', for both subjects are hot properties in the world of collecting. In British hearts, it appears, cats and dogs share equal billing with the monarchy. Furthermore, American buyers are to the forefront for all things canine and feline; and the Japanese have joined the chase.

The connection between royalty and pets runs deep. The royals have had a noticeable effect on the popularity of dog breeds, from Queen Victoria's regard for her champion white collie, Snowball, to Queen Elizabeth II's love of corgis. The trend for royal corgis was begun by George VI, who acquired one in 1933 when he was Duke of York. By the time of his coronation in 1937 the popularity of the corgi had risen from fifteenth to fifth position among the non-sporting breeds. In the secluded, seldom-used grounds of Marlborough House on the Mall in London to this day is preserved a remarkable pet cemetery where four-legged loved ones of the royal families have been buried.

In 1988, at the time of Crufts, the annual dog jamboree in London, *The Times* quoted an animal psychiatrist as saying: 'People bring the dog into the family truly as a member of the family. In the old days dogs were quite distinctive from humans but today people cease to see their dog as a dog.' Sir Edwin Landseer, the great Victorian animal painter, beloved of his queen, would disagree with part of that statement. If the homily were applied to cats, the artist Louis Wain, a couple of nineteenth century generations later than Landseer, would equally demur. 'In the old days' Landseer responded to the Victorians' attitude to dogs by imbuing his canine portraits with characteristics that were subtly human; Wain, who drew cats even after an onset of madness, went much further, turning his cats into human beings (or human beings into cats, if you wish), dressed in clothes and occupied in the activities of people. (See chapters 2 and 4).

Paintings are just part of a large field which covers cat and dog collectables. A porcelain hound from a 200-year-old Chinese dynasty can easily bound into five figures in the saleroom, which is twice as much as he might make if he were a heron or a rabbit. Cats

Victorian painter Ada Elizabeth Tucker struck a vein of picture appeal that is as rich today as it was in her own times. This picture is entitled, 'What can it be?'

perform equally well. A bright-eyed, foot-high beauty by Gallé, the French glass master, makes thousands. A fingernail-size lead figure of a farmyard 'spiteful cat', arch-backed and spitting, by Britain's, the toy soldier maker, has changed hands at £15/$24, a phenomenal advance on his price of sixpence when new in the 1950s. An 8cm (3in) painted bronze feline, playing the violin Wain-style, hailing from Vienna at the turn of the century, can make £200-£300/$320-$480.

The fever for collecting dogs and cats cannot be separated from the cultural and social climate around us. Two happenings, one nightly, the other yearly, sum up this passion: the stage musical *Cats*, and the Crufts dog show.

Bookings for *Cats* at the New London Theatre in Drury Lane, London, stretch beyond the year 2000. Statistics (perhaps the term is catistics?) abound. Every evening, the dancers prance the equivalent of 18 miles. The show has opened in fifteen countries, and by September 1987 it had already taken £200 million/$320 million at box offices around the world. Its creator, Andrew Lloyd Webber, has become a millionaire several times over. Royalty flocks to the show. Princess Margaret is a regular, but the Prince of Wales has been

the most demonstrative. A member of the cast retailed this account to a newspaper: 'We gave a little reception which Prince Charles attended after the show. When he was asked which was his favourite cat onstage, he said, "The one who did this," then he went down in a perfect splits.' Lloyd Webber based his musical on poems by T.S. Eliot, including the work, *Old Possum's Book of Practical Cats*. Each cat has been given a definite persona — and students of Louis Wain avow that there is more than a touch of the old, mad cat man in the characterization. Perhaps it is not entirely coincidental that Wain's works have boomed in collecting

terms since the show opened in April 1981.

Crufts is named after Charles Cruft (1852-1938), who began to organize dog shows as a natural offshoot from his career in dog food. The 1988 show, the ninety-second, attracted 15,557 entries and the supreme champion was a three-year-old English setter, Sh Ch Starlite Express of Valsett. Columns of newsprint are filled every year about the competitions and the backstage dramas at Crufts; 1988 was no exception. No collector of ephemera dealing with the canine species can afford to miss this pearl of doggy lore, by Sally Brompton in *The Times*, describing the experiences of the

Kittenish activity in another typical work by Horatio Henry Couldrey. He called this painting of 1890 'A Narrow Escape'.

previous year's supreme champion, the Afghan, Viscount Grant, known to his friends as Gable:

'Life has not necessarily been a bed of marrow-bones for Gable in these past 12 months... Fame has its limitations, and he could not honestly say that success had not changed him. Even his master noticed that he had become more

Design for a Christmas card by Louis Wain, the artist who went mad drawing cats.

I Sing my Christmas Greeting to you.

louis Wain.

aloof and insular — less inclined to hurl himself gleefully at visitors. Just walking down the street had become a problem, what with people recognizing him from his pictures and television commercials. Cars screeched to a halt, doors slammed and, frankly, the whole thing was turning him into a nervous wreck.'

From Viscount Grant's memoirs to the mawkish tale of royal Caesar, from Landseer's monarchic mastiffs to faithful old Pluto and the *nouveau riche* Snoopy, from Felix to television's alley toms, from snooty Ming aristocats to cheerfully somersaulting moggies of a new, electronic Orient...cats and dogs are for collectors of all seasons.

My heart is with you to-night.

Chapter Two

LANDSEER'S DOGS

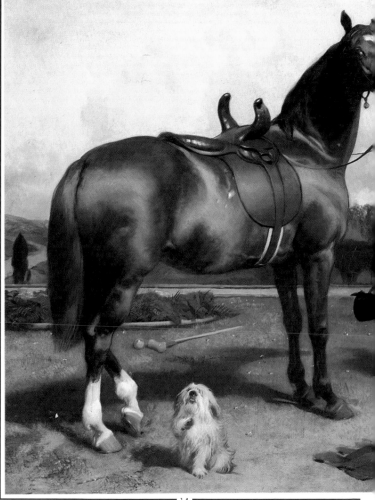

Sir Edwin Landseer demonstrates his flair for capturing the essence of the dog in paint. He called his canvas 'Prosperity'. His canine works are among the frontrunners of Victorian art.

The collectors of Sir Edwin Landseer (1802-1873) could hold an artistic Crufts of their own. An archpriest of nineteenth century genre painting (a branch of art invariably linked with the word 'sentimental'), he made dogs a species of his own and the canine world a Landseer fiefdom over which he ruled, patronized by his monarch and rewarded with adoring tribute from the great Victorian public.

Discussing one of his paintings, Christopher Forbes has written*: 'The dogs are not only beautiful, but also alert, sensitive and intelligent; each is shown in a separate position and in an attitude that seems to reflect his individual state of mind. Following the lead of Sir Thomas Lawrence (1769-1830) and other Romantic portraitists, Landseer shows us not only what *his* sitters looked like, but by the tilt of a head or the glitter of an eye gives us a glimpse into their inner personalities.' As a 'sitter', what more could man's best friend ask? Much of that which came later in dog art borrows heavily from Landseer.

He was the son of a London engraver, John Landseer, and two of his brothers, Charles and Thomas, were also artists. Edwin was a child prodigy. At the age of 13, it is recalled, he spotted in the

The deerhounds bear such strong comparison with the work of Sir Edwin Landseer that opinion attributes this study of a Scottish ghillie and companions to the celebrated Victorian painter and 'another hand'. At Bonhams in 1987 the buyer had sufficient faith in the master's contribution to pay £10,000/$16,000.

street a strange breed of dog, unknown in London. He raced from his home and begged the owner to allow him to paint it. The picture of an Alpine mastiff is with us today, a lively and stunningly competent work of art which is highly prized as an example of his earlier achievements.

Landseer had made his debut at the Royal Academy's annual exhibition at the age of 12, with two small paintings, one of dogs and one of a mule. Because of his talent for drawing animals, especially dogs, Henry Fuseli, in charge of drawing classes at the Academy, called him 'my little dog boy'. The young painter applied himself diligently to the study of anatomy and his early drawings of horses are skilful and lifelike. He was elected an Associate of the Royal Academy at the age of 24, the youngest possible age. In 1874, the year after his death, the Academy was to honour him with a retrospective exhibition of his work, the first one-man show to be held in those august halls.

Landseer's preoccupation with the Highlands of Scotland (a passion that was to produce his celebrated and prolifically reproduced *Stag at Bay*) was already established when Queen Victoria began to invite him as a guest on the royal estates. She showed him great favouritism and commanded him to paint many

In the entrance hall of Phillips in London hangs this painting of the firm's founder, Harry Phillips, with Friend, the dog that saved him from drowning in the eighteenth century.

pictures of her dogs and children. Occasionally he would give her and her husband, Prince Albert, painting lessons and the royal pair occasionally commissioned him to make paintings and drawings to be presented as gifts to one another.

A remarkable 'pets family album' painting, *Queen Victoria's Favourite Dogs and Parrot*, also known as *The Royal Pets*, was exhibited at the Academy in 1838, the exhibition being the first which Victoria had viewed at the Academy as queen. Two years earlier, her mother, the Duchess of Kent, had presented her with a Landseer portrait of her spaniel, Dash. In the group painting, Dash reclined in regal splendour on an embroidered velvet hassock in the company of two other royal dogs, Hester and Nero, and the parrot Lorey. The spaniel, posed on his own little 'throne', was much copied, not the least in needlework on samplers, cushion-coverings and firescreens.

Given Landseer's fame and his royal support, it was not unusual for his paintings to appear in other media. His 1839 Academy success was *A Jack in Office*, a triumph of high Victorian pop art which showed a fat, well-fed Jack Russell guarding his master's meat cart from the depredations of other dogs, including a pointer bitch, a poodle and a scruffy terrier. Two years later the painting became the model for a

*The Royal Academy (1837-1901) Revisited, Victorian Paintings from the Forbes Magazine Collection.

political cartoon when the Conservative administration fell, and 'Jack', Lord John Russell, became Leader of the House of Commons and Home Secretary — and thus a dispenser of patronage. The caricaturist 'H.B.', or John Doyle, parodied Landseer's composition in a cartoon with a vigilant Lord John Russell on the cart; Lord Brougham, hungry for office, as the predatory pointer; O'Connell sitting up and begging as the poodle; and Lord Durham depicted as the scruffy, marauding terrier.

Victorian foxhounds in a barn, painted by John Emms. A charming study in the £600-£800/$960-$1,280 class.

Critics' opinions of Landseer's work varied, but none could gainsay his way with dogs. William Makepeace Thackeray, in an article in the form of a letter from his alter ego, M.A. Titmarsh, to Monsieur Anatole Victor Isidor Hyacinthe Achille Hercule de Bricabrac, observed that the dogs-and-parrot painting was Landseer's best picture in the 1838 exhibition, but added: 'I do not think he understands how to paint the great beast, man, quite so well...They [Landseer's paintings] are, if you like, the most dexterous pictures that ever were painted, but not great pictures.'

Queen Victoria's regard for Landseer was unqualified. After his death, she wrote in her diary a tribute to her 'kind old friend': 'How many an incident do I remember, connected with Landseer! He kindly has shown me how to draw stags' heads, and how to draw in chalks, but I could never manage that well. I possess thirty-nine oil paintings of his, sixteen chalk drawings (framed), two frescoes, and many sketches.'

In addition, Landseer has left his legacy in many public collections. The Victoria and Albert Museum has 21 oils of his and many drawings — and, of course, on the most visible public level, Trafalgar Square in the heart of London is guarded by his celebrated lions.

Landseer's name conjures up images of dogs as the epitome of faithfulness, custodians with cold wet noses and shaggy coats, but showing a gleam of stern character in their eye. On the subject of *The Royal Pets*, Christopher Forbes wrote: 'While

Harry Phillips's Dog Friend is remembered for his bravery and resource in a Victorian papier-mâché table, and other artefacts.

Landseer has not endowed these creatures with specifically human characteristics, as he was to do in many of his most famous pictures, such as *Dignity and Impudence*, exhibited at the British Institution in 1831 (Tate Gallery), there is a suggestion of the animals' mental activity, which makes Landseer's painting quite different from, say, portraits of horses by George Stubbs.'

A considerably more light-hearted approach was taken by another highly successful Victorian painter of dogs who exhibited at the Royal Academy,

John Hayes, who flourished in the 1890s, painted dogs from life and with life. 'Fun' genre pictures such as this, 'A Vain Appeal', are hugely in demand.

The inimitable Gourlay Steell, painter of the Scottish animal scene, 'The Elder's Collie' is a magnificent example of his work, dates from 1883, and sold for £5,500/$8,800 in 1980.

William Henry Hamilton Trood (1860-1899), whose pictures glory in titles with a decidedly popular ring: *A Coveted Bone, The Old Man's Darling, Home Sweet Home*, and so on. Trood, who had a prolific canine output, is often the star of the Bonhams annual auctions of dogs in art, and his prices are racing helter-skelter up the scale, placing his works in a range accessible only to the wealthy and devoted collectors or those with a beady eye on investment prospects.

Examine one of his more coveted works, *Hot Pursuit*, and you begin to understand the chemistry of Trood's genius in painting dogs for a popular, pet-loving public. It is a large canvas, 71cm x 160cm (26in x 63in), dated 1894, a broad field which Trood filled with canine jollity. The scene involves a central group of animals engaged in a wild chase through a barn, watched in varying degrees of fascination, wonderment, awe and alarm by as many as 30 other dogs, representing many breeds. Here are dogs for all seasons. Each spectator is finely and accurately drawn, a lively vignette of dog art. Trood's pictures demonstrate very clearly that it's fun being a dog.

Chapter Three

IN THE
PICTURE

Dogs have appeared in paintings from early times but it was not until the nineteenth century, with its rise of new monied classes and the development of the Victorian attitudes to hearth and home, that the dog in art was sentimentalized. Before Victorian days, the dog had a strictly regulated niche in art. It was mainly to be found in the sporting scene, with carefully controlled appearances at the foot of the master on other occasions. Through the centuries, however, there has been a tradition of painting the pets of kings and queens. The 'chocolate box' vogue for painting dogs peaked around the end of the nineteenth century, but it has found a new lease of life in modern painting. As long as there is a market for a genre, commercially-minded artists will be found working in that genre. Cats, totally lacking the work ethic, took more time than dogs to achieve artistic eminence. Once having been established, in mid to late-Victorian days, as popular and rewarding 'sitters', they have never looked back.

Significantly, in the 1988 annual Bonhams sale of dogs and cats in art (timed in February to coincide with Crufts) the top price of £30,000/$54,000 was paid not for a canine subject, but for a painting of a kitten peering into a looking glass, with the schmaltzy title of *Who's the Fairest of Them All?*. It was painted by Frank Paton, a far from front-rank artist, in 1883, fairly early for cat genre pictures, and the price was some five times the estimate. 'I think the subject, rather than the artist, accounted for the price,' an official of the auction house said laconically.

Artists to watch out for in the kennel stakes — include Liverpool's Charles Towne and Richard Ansdell, Melton Mowbray's John Ferneley, and from this century the popular Cecil Aldin and Arthur Wardle. George W. Horlor was a popular animal painter who exhibited between 1849 and 1891. He lived in Birmingham, Cheltenham and Brentford and had 18 pictures in Royal Academy exhibitions between 1854 and 1890. George Armfield (typical titles, *At Rest, Catching the Scent, Dinner Time*) made a career out of painting dogs. Others, such as Gourlay Steell, are collected not only for their dog paintings, but for masterly, powerful portraits of farm animals, notably some impressive denizens of noble Scottish herds. Nearer our own times, Maud Earl, who died in 1943, was the daughter of George Earl, a well-known animal painter. Her speciality was dogs and she painted the pets of both Queen Victoria and Edward VII. A dog painting of hers — say, *Supper*

Victorian man's faithful friend. 'Guarding the Day's Catch', by John Morris, a popular painter of such scenes. This one sold for £420/$672 in 1988.

Time, depicting a Scottish terrier seated by an empty bowl — can be in the £6,000-plus ($9,600) bracket and outclass a dog work by her father.

Prices for dog and cat paintings have continued to rise through the 1980s. Primitive paintings of dogs — by untrained artists — have a particular naive appeal of their own, and their values have increased by leaps and bounds, thanks largely to interest from American collectors. In recent years portraits of unknown (human) sitters by minor artists have taken on a shine; one theory is that they are being bought by yuppies to hang on their walls as 'instant ancestors'. Perhaps there is a similar development in canine portrait painting: are the new rich buying the primitives as 'instant ancestral dogs'?

Chapter Four

MAD ABOUT CATS

Think of cat pictures, think of Louis Wain. When the artist died in 1939, mad, sad and almost forgotten, one account estimated that he had produced 150,000 drawings for the record, the majority of them images of cats. There are Wain drawings yet undiscovered, for he was a prolific sketcher and generous with his extempore works. Those that are in circulation are traded expensively: watercolours and drawings, originals for postcards and the postcards themselves, vignettes to illustrate picture stories and the books themselves, illustrations for calendars, menu cards, advertisements and packaging. Wain turned cats into humans — or, as often happens, humans into cats, as we shall see. H. G. Wells, in a tribute written for an appeal in 1927 when the artist was sick and in need, observed: 'He invented a cat style, a cat society, a whole cat world. English cats that do not look like Louis Wain cats are ashamed of themselves.' It is an appropriate epitaph for the man whose name means cats.

His art was not always devoted to cats, however. Indeed, his first published drawing was on the subject of birds. This was in 1881 when the Christmas number of *Illustrated Sporting and Dramatic News* published a Wain drawing of bullfinches, miscaptioned 'robins' much to the artist's embarrassment. And, for a time, dogs were the basis of his earnings as he worked in London, sketching prize-winning animals for *Illustrated* and, especially, *Stock Keeper*.

Wain was born in 1860. He was sickly, had a hare lip and always laboured under a feeling of inferiority. Nevertheless, he considered himself a man of many parts — artist, scientist, musician and poet; it is said that he once offered an opera to Sir Henry Wood, but the opus is forgotten by posterity; as a writer his talents were of the dimmest, as is proved by some banal contributions to *Windsor Magazine* in the 1890s. The off-beat and the abstract attracted him, but owing to the early death of his father, and after art-school training, he had to apply himself to the hard realities of helping to support his mother and five sisters by his drawing abilities.

In 1884 he insisted, against family opposition, on marrying a governess in his mother's household, 10 years his senior. The marriage was happy, but his wife was stricken with cancer and died childless in 1887. Wain's sisters had given the couple a kitten called Peter, and during the long hours of vigil at his wife's

Wain at work illustrating a 1902 book on cats and dogs.

Left: Wain's work touched many aspects of art, promotion and commerce. This gem is an illustration done for the panels on the side of a box of Mazawattee tea, a scrap worth £50-£100/$80-$160.

Below Left: A Wain cover for a Raphel Tuck story book which included inside plates by the artist.

bedside Wain took to sketching the cat. He came to know more about the thinking and movements of cats than any other animal. 'With my wife invalided to the house, [Peter] never suffered inattention, loneliness or thoughtlessness,' Wain later recalled. 'His was the genius which gilded many a sorrowful hour, and lightened many a burden. To him properly belongs the foundation of my career.'

Through the relationship with Peter, he moved away from dog drawings — although these were the better sellers in the late-Victorian society — and filled sketchbooks with portraits of his pet, now invested with human attributes. And something more than human attributes: cats he saw as cure-alls for a wide variety of physical and psychological debilities. Was this the beginning of Wain's progress to the stage where he was 'mad about cats'? Of Peter, he told an interviewer: 'He has helped me to wipe out, once and for all, the contempt in which the cat has been held in this country, and raised its status from the questionable care and affection of the old maid to a real and permanent place in the home. I have myself found, as a result of many years of inquiry and study, that all people who keep cats, and are in the habit of nursing them, do not suffer from those petty little ailments which all flesh is heir to, *viz*, nervous complaints of a minor sort. Hysteria and rheumatism, too, are unknown, and all lovers of "pussy" are of the sweetest temperament.'

In 1886 Wain illustrated *Madame Tabby's Establishment* for Macmillan. In this book, however, his cat style was not yet perfected. When the Victoria and Albert Museum exhibited Wain's works in 1972, a catalogue assessment by Bryan Reade contained this criticism of *Madame Tabby's* drawings: 'It must be admitted that here and there a pedigree Persian is found looking as though it had been drawn over the guide lines for a Peke or Yorkshire terrier' After the Macmillan commisson, Wain went on to provide a feline blockbuster for a Christmas issue of *The Illustrated London News*: 10 panels containing more than 150 cats. After that, cats were to be his life and livelihood; requests for his work multiplied.

He veered between dressed and undressed cats. Sometimes

he drew cats simply as cats. Mainly, however, he is remembered for his animals engaging in human activities, courting one another in flirtatious poses, delivering after-dinner speeches (*very* Victorian), teaching, and wearing a monocle to read a newspaper or pen a letter, playing musical instruments, cats by the seaside, at the opera, out shopping, at home cooking. What did his eye see as he prepared a sketch for a more elaborate drawing? One of

'The Happy Couple', Wain at his wryest in a gouache, one of the many illustrations produced in his long years of drawing cats (Bonhams).

his remarks seems to hint that, often, he turned human beings into cats, rather than the other way round: 'I take a sketch-book to a restaurant or other public place, and draw the people in their different positions as *cats*, getting as near to their human characteristics as possible. This gives me *doubly* nature, and these studies I think my best humerous work.' Clearly, such a technique, to be successful, would depend on a skilful ability to portray feline physiognomy,

'Cat Reading', a gouache by Louis Wain, sold at Bonhams in 1988 for £660/$1056.

acquired through hours of sketching Peter and other animals in life.

In the first decade of the new century, Wain was enormously well known for his cat art, a truly household name. He arguably contributed more than any other single person to the British passion for keeping cats as domestic pets, promoting them to the status of valued members of the family, cats of character and personality. At Westgate-on-Sea, Kent, where he now lived with his mother and unmarried sister, he was sought for press interviews and bombarded with questions on all aspects of that great topic, cats. Amid much commonsense, he communicated some strange beliefs: cats have a tendency to travel north, and face north as a magnet does; cats are mobile lightning conductors and clean themselves to complete an electrical circuit.

He was producing drawings at a rate approaching two every day for reproduction on postcards, in books and magazines, and in his own *Louis Wain's Annual*, which came out at intervals between 1901 and 1921. He could do a fast

cat sketch in 45 seconds — and made hundreds of them, which he handed out, willy-nilly to his friends, relatives or people he met in everyday life. Examples must exist today in substantial quantities, with or without his characteristic and clear signature, grist for the collecting mill. Indeed, the prolificness of his output led to piracy by unscrupulous publishers and a glut of his drawings. The latter factor, coupled with a drop in publishing demand during the first world war, signalled the end of Wain's heyday. An accident in

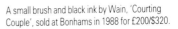

A small brush and black ink by Wain, 'Courting Couple', sold at Bonhams in 1988 for £200/$320.

1914 — he was concussed by a fall from a bus — and the death of his eldest sister in 1917 contributed to a deterioration of his mental and physical health. There was a brief flirtation with 'futurist cats' in ceramics, but his entire stock is said to have been lost in the sinking of a cargo boat. His drawings of the early Twenties reveal a preoccupation with patterns of wallpaper and furniture at the expense of the glorious Wain cat. Something was sadly wrong. He began to suffer from acute paranoia, and in 1924 he was certified insane.

In madness, he drew to the end — weird abstract cats, often no more than a pair of feline eyes, burning through slabs of colour in geometrical shapes. A fund was started to rescue Wain from the paupers' ward of an asylum for the insane. In the Thirties, however, it seemed that few were concerned with the fate of 'the mad cat man'. He died in 1939.

Through the ensuing war and the immediate post-war era, Wain's art languished in the doldrums. The 1970s and 80s have seen it receive a massive fillip. Wain is the subject of frequent exhibitions. His original works reach hundreds and thousands at auction, depending on nature, subject and matter and size. His cats — Victorian damsels, Edwardian stage-door Johnnies, wartime soldier lads — are up among the old masters. Wain postcard pussies are purring with satisfaction: they are bracketed with some of the most sought-after subjects in that collecting field. Who knows how many undiscovered Wain cats are lying sleeping in attics, trunks and cupboards? For them all, welcome is writ large on the mat.

The incomparable work of Louis Wain, seen here in a postcard — good, jolly fun by a master of the art. Early postcards start at under £5/$8; original artwork can run into thousands.

Chapter Five

CERAMIC CATS

Those who will not hear (or read) a bad word said (or written) about cats are advised to steel themselves against some calumnies on the feline species which, alas, this chapter must acknowledge as a matter of historical record. Cat lovers have been warned.

For thousands of years the cat has been adored by many and worshipped as a god by a few. Bronze cats of ancient Egypt are highly prized. China has left us a heritage of magnificent porcelain and bronze cats. In Japan cats were so esteemed that the work of keeping down mice was considered beneath their dignity. People painted cats on doors and bought cats of bronze, wood and ceramic to scare away the mice. Thus old Japan was overrun with rodents and endowed with a wealth of beautiful cat objects. Cats modelled as cast-iron doorstoppers — desirable collectables in the present day — guarded many a nineteenth-century American home thanks, reputedly, to their powers of being able to ward off evil. So far, so good. Now, here comes the bad news from Europe.

It was not until surprisingly late in time, the middle of the eighteenth century, that the first English porcelain cats were produced in sufficient quantity to

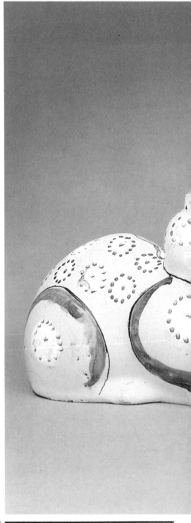

From northern France in the early eighteenth century comes this pair of faience cats, round and friendly. The mouths are pierced to form ewers. In the £1,000/$1,600 class.

be around still today. Even then, and for some considerable time later, there was a dearth of cheaper, pottery cats. The blame is put on superstition. Cats, inscrutable, independent, unpredictable, did not have a happy place in country lore. Records of the Chelmsford witch trials of 1566 make mention of 'Sathan' in the likeness of a white spotted cat, and there are other socio-historic and folkloric references to cats similarly perceived.

John Skelton (c.1460-1529), recipient of the academic distinction of 'poet-laureate' from the universities of Oxford, Cambridge and Louvain, and tutor to Prince Henry (Henry VIII),

An attractive china money bank dating from the period between World Wars One and Two.

undoubtedly knew his public when he wrote: 'Vengeance I ask and cry, / By way of exclamation, / On the whole of the nation / Of cattes wild and tame: / God send them sorrow and shame!' The record nevertheless reveals a personal reason for his extreme stance:

'O cat of churlish kind, / The fiend was in thy mind / When thou my bird untwined!' On the whole, however, while dogs were regarded with affection (and their images welcomed on the mantelshelf), cats in country areas were met with distrust, unease or often downright fear.

Eighteenth-century porcelain cats appear to have existed in greater numbers than those of

An unusual Staffordshire salt-glazed 'agate' cat demonstrating that it can live down its witchcraft reputation by keeping the mice nuisance under control. It dates from about 1745 and this 12cm (5in) figure might reasonably attract a £2,000/$3,200 bid at auction.

pottery cats: the theory is that those who bought porcelain would be wealthier, therefore more educated and less superstitious than the purchasers of pottery. There is, however, a bonus in this for the pottery collector who likes his or her cats round and cuddly. While the makers of porcelain animals were prepared to create fairly realistic and accurate figures — the rangy, mouse-devouring felines of the eighteenth century — the potters leaned towards reassuringly plump and cheerful animals that would pose no threat to the domestic hearth. They were cats totally unfitted to be a witch's companion; none of your sinuous, satanic overtones here.

Some of the earliest English porcelain cats were produced by the London Factory of Chelsea in the 1750/60s. Sometimes, they formed part of a larger tableau: an example is a candlestick which has a terrier attacking a fox while a frightened cat climbs a vine. From this time and source there

These small models are made in bronze and then painted, many of them not much more than 4cm (1.5in) in height.

are also tiny toys, and scent bottles known as seals. One scent bottle depicts a cat holding a mouse, the cat's head forming the stopper; another has a cat climbing foliage in pursuit of doves. Many of these seals have French mottoes and may have been inspired by similar artefacts from Mennecy in France.

Physical realism in porcelain is represented in a Bow group of around 1770 in which a cat holds a dead mouse to its lips, while a second mouse is seen running to the safety of a hole in a mound. The colouring is another matter: our cat hero is resplendent in purple and gold. At that early period it was difficult to achieve realism, especially on a small scale. (The squabby shapes produced by the potters arguably owed as much to the market price of skills as to the public's superstitious aversion to cat-like cats!) By the early years of the nineteenth century, however, models of cats became more true to life. By 1820, Derby was able to

offer a very convincing group which showed a woman stroking a grey cat in her lap, while her lover offers a morsel of food to his pug. Both animals wear the gilded collars often seen on porcelain cats.

Many collectors concentrate wholly on the more naively-fashioned porcelain of the early years. Others go for the developed wares of Derby, Worcester and Rockingham. Rockingham cats are most keenly collected from the 1820s and 30s. The majority of the true-bred ones are marked, often with the initials CL and a number incised on the base. Other markings include the legend, 'Rockingham Works, Bramfield', accompanied by an impressed griffin. Although produced in large quantities, Rockingham cats are scarce today. Many non-Rockingham models of Staffordshire origin have been confidently but wrongly described as Rockingham. In the cat jungle, it behoves a potential buyer to deal

with an established and reputable dealer, and to read the auction catalogue carefully. The most desirable Rockingham cats are rarely more than 10cm (4in) in height, and most of them measure only about 5cm (2in). They were often made sitting on modelled cushions. One cat resting in a basket with her kittens was made as a pair to a bitch with her puppies.

Henry Sandon, the respected authority on porcelain, especially Worcester, observed in the magazine, *Art & Antiques Weekly* *(Clues for Cat Collectors*, 5 December, 1980): 'Like Swansea, Chamberlain Worcester, Grainger Worcester, Bloor Derby and Sampson Hancock Derby, they [Rockingham] also produced fat cats hollow under the base with little feet sticking out in front. These are found with different coloured spots or as marmalade cats, or even tabbies and greys.

'Perhaps more beautiful, and usually better modelled, are those found sitting on cushions. The Chamberlain Worcester ones are often shown on a matt blue ground cushion and they will almost invariably be marked inside the base in script with the words *Chamberlain Worcester*. Cats on cushions from the other Worcester factory will usually have the factory mark impressed under the glaze in block letters, *Grainger Lee & Co Worcester*, and this mark is sometimes very difficult to read, the bone china body and the glaze being very white. Many other English factories making bone china in the period 1820-50 made similar cat models and these are seldom marked. So it becomes a very difficult task to tell who made them. The collector is on much safer ground with the wares of the last half of the nineteenth and this century as the

Dynastic cat. A fragmentary Egyptian bronze figure of a cat, 24cm (9½in) high. £5,800/$9,280 in the middle 1980s.

better factories invariably marked them.'

In his survey, Henry Sandon opined that perhaps the finest English cat group came from Worcester. Modelled by James Hadley and first made in 1875, it shows a mother with three kittens. One of these looks out enquiringly on the new world from a safe spot under the mother's stomach, one plays with her tail, and the third pulls at her face. 'The group is quite a rare one, perhaps as rare as the Chelsea seals, but the serious collector of cats should try to obtain one.'

What of the cat *potters*? Decoration of a deliberately unrealistic manner, it seems, was one of the conditions of acceptability. Who could suspect sinister attributes in a house cat with cheerful purple and blue stripes on his limbs? Thus was painted one of the earliest pottery models, a small seated cat from Lambeth in 1676.

Earthenware cats were often decorated by a process known as slip-marbling. Washes of slip — a

Although small in stature these cold painted bronze cats from Vienna can reach hundreds of pounds or dollars at auction.

thin paste of clay, water and pigment — were painted in lines, or simply splashed, on the model. A marbled pattern was achieved by drawing a comb across the wet colours. Similar effects were obtained with a sponge. It was an ideal method for use on the rounded, simple pottery figures. Thomas Whieldon, who set up as a potter in 1740, developed a technique to produce 'agate ware', resulting in small cats which gave the impression they were made of the semi-precious stone. Another of his tricks was taken up by many Staffordshire potters who wanted to cash in on the tortoiseshell look.

As attitudes towards cats changed, the potters became more daring. White bisque cats, imported into Britain from Germany in the nineteenth century, are realistic-looking models. Anthropomorphic themes became popular. Cats in all manner of poses appeared sporting heraldic designs following the onset of the craze for collecting small objects representing the coats of arms of British cities and seaside resorts. In the twentieth century, felines continue to pour out of the pottery and porcelain factories, ranging from exclusive cats in expensive limited editions, to mass-produced models by the battalion.

Chapter Six

CERAMIC DOGS

Dedicated admirers of the dog will thoroughly approve of a series of Victorian mugs whose decoration was designed to benefit junior's education. They are ABC mugs, with an interesting outlook on alphabetical priorities. D is obvious enough: it represents, exclusively, Dog, 'the friend of the House', and comes in blue. What about B, brown-coloured? B stands for Butcher, but a butcher who, you might have guessed, kept a 'Great Dog'. In like vein the Victorian potter goes through the alphabet, finding, at any cost to logic, canine opportunities: P is for Park, Peacock, Parrot and Puppy; H is for Horse, House, Hound, Horn; and so on. The dogs appear in a variety of scenic settings, domestic and pastoral. Are there really 26 mugs in the set? Who knows? What a challenge to the potter's lexicographical gymnastics, and what a challenge to a modern day collector to seek the whole range.

Ceramic dogs did not suffer from the superstitious hang-ups that restrained the style of pottery cats in the eighteenth century. Man's best friend was in demand in a large number of forms ranging from the ultra-realistic to the near-abstract (although the latter probably owed its being to lack of modelling skills rather than conscious intent). It was as if Europe agreed with the words of Frederick the Great: 'The more I see of men the better I like my dog.'

From Whieldon pottery in 1775-60 came an animal, some three and a half inches in height, which is the subject of debate: cat or dog? The balance of probability comes down on the side of the latter view. It is a rare piece, decorated with the mottled brown glaze typical of Whieldon ware, and easily leaps well into four

Japanese cats beware. This fierce but beautiful Arita model of a dog dates from the seventeenth century and is 24cm (9½in) in height. In 1987 it sold at auction for £7,700/$12.320.

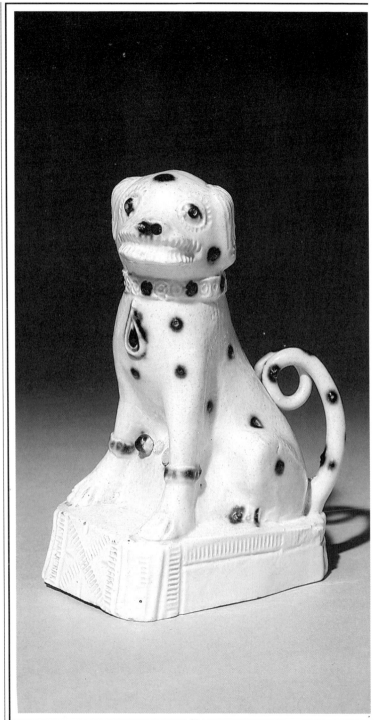

A guard dog with spots. This salt-glazed ceramic model of a 'Dog of Fo', after a Chinese original, dates from about 1750 and is in the £4,000-£5,000/ $6,400-$8,000 class.

figures when it appears at auction on either side of the Atlantic. Around the same time, the London Derby factory was producing its famous scent bottles, or seals, modelled with dog images: one shows a dalmation skirmishing with a cat and the lugubrious legend, *Il Mort Doucement*. Other dogs frolic around the bases of small Derby candlesticks and spill-holders, generously and thoughtfully decorated with tree stumps, if not lamp-posts. Some of Derby's output had a realism ahead of its time. A porcelain figure of a pug dog of 1770-75 sits in repose, an easily recognizable breed. From around 1820, Chamberlain Worcester porcelain figures of whippets, a pair lying with forepaws elegantly crossed, are highly prized, and again they are very lifelike.

Staffordshire dogs are widely collected and in fairly generous supply. Where would antique fairs be without this cheerful breed? They include the ever popular pair of china spaniels, dating from the mid-nineteenth century and known as 'comforters' presumably because their owner never felt alone. A rarer model of the nineteenth century is an aristocratic-looking 28cm (11in) high animal, taken to be a borzoi

— a breed which first became popular in Britain around the middle of the century. Modern reproductions of Staffordshire dogs abound, but the genuine animals are keenly sought, and a pair can fetch anything from £100/$160 upwards, with rare examples well above the four-figure mark. Collectors are always on the lookout for Staffordshire dogs that 'do things', such as a reclining dog of 1860 which is not only decorative but doubles as a spillholder in that the tree stump behind him is hollowed.

Novelties exist from other factories. Derby produced some very desirable porcelain heads of dogs, Dalmatians among them, which are whistles. Fragility and time have taken their toll of these whistles, and an example of around 1800 would cost between £300-£400/$480-$640 in pristine condition. There are also nineteenth century brown-glazed pottery furniture supports (for raising a sideboard, piano or a heavy chair above the ground), modelled as spaniel heads; obviously, a complement of four is ideally required by a collector. And from Germany in the late nineteenth century came pottery table match-strikers in box form, glazed coppery brown to simulate

Far right top: It stands hardly 8.5cm (3½in) in height, yet its price topped £5,000/$8,000 at auction in 1986. It is a Staffordshire salt-glazed pug, probably enamelled in London.

Far right bottom: Part of the menagerie of an American fairground carousel, this greyhound would have whirled round in the 1890s in the company of gaily decorated prancing horses. Today it is a rare collectors' item with a price of £33,750/$54,000 on its head.

Below: A pair of faience models of hounds, probably Brussels, dating from the early eighteenth century. The figures are pierced to form money boxes; 23cm (9in), sold for £10,000/$16,000 in the early 1980s. A treasured item.

wood colouring and often depicting gun dogs at work in the countryside.

Many a Victorian parlour had, seated by the fireplace, a life-size terracotta model, painted realistically to represent a pug, terrier, spaniel or bulldog. 'Flatback' figures of setters in green glass, which would have a purely decorative function in a bookcase or on a mantelshelf, are fairly rare survivors of the nineteenth century, although burnished cast-iron examples are relatively common. The appearance of dogs (or cats, for that matter) on tableware tends to put a premium on the price. A George IV Staffordshire blue and white serving platter, some 36cm (14in) in length, might sell for about £100/$160 in a general antique shop if the central scene, surrounded by a border of flowers, is a simple countryside view; should one depict dogs as its central feature, however, the

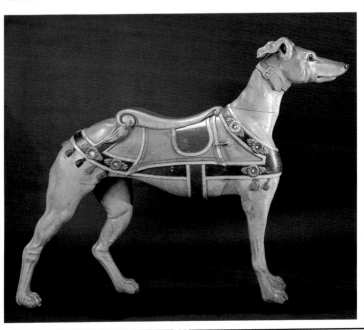

Right: A pair of Derbyshire salt-glazed stoneware spaniels, dating from around 1840, 38cm (15in) high; £2,000-£3,000/$3,200-$4,800.

Below: Various canine figures make their appearance among companion animals from the Royal Doulton character stable.

object immediately moves up into the 'doggy' specialization area of dealing, and the price can easily be doubled. A dinner service with such a theme would be a major item of expense.

In the twentieth century, the Royal Doulton bulldog goes from strength to strength, as befits the symbol of British rectitude and substance. For light relief we have 'Bonzo' dog serving as a jug; a bemused-looking spaniel which can be illuminated electrically as a night-light; 'Dismal Desmond', a cartoon character who doubles as a jar (lift his doleful head for access); and any number of Disney and Snoopy dogs gone to pot.

Chapter Seven

TOP CATS

Cats have been used to advertise a wide range of commodities from milk (obviously) to high-performance motor fuel. Advertising ephemera is high among the priorities of many cat collectors. No commercial artist employed cats as skillfully, effectively and lovingly as Théophile Alexandre Steinlen (1859-1923), who arrived to work in Paris from his native Switzerland in 1882. In an extremely prolific career he illustrated about 100 books and more than 1,000 issues of periodicals, but it is his 50 or so posters which command the most attention from collectors today, with prime examples selling for many thousands of dollars in New York where poster interest is most keen.

Jane Abdy (*The French Poster*, New York, 1969) writes: 'Steinlen was one of the four or five great poster artists of his time; all his lithographic work is distinguished by a freshness and vigour which makes it powerful, and a simplicity and sympathy which makes it appealing. Little of Steinlen's compassion for the poor, which runs through the rest of his work like a shrill note, is stressed in his posters. The subjects of his posters are those dearest to his heart, his pretty little daughter Colette, and his beloved cats.'

Cats filled Steinlen's home, and his pictures. He turned to cats to promote the sales of sterilized milk — he has three of them seated at the feet of Colette, who sips at a bowl, in a poster generally hailed as among his very best. Equally, he recruited to them to lend grace and elegance to a poster advertising an exhibition of contemporary paintings and drawings in 1894. Nor was he averse to amusing deployment of a cat to proclaim

Steinlen again, at home with cats, this time in a poster for a Paris art exhibition.

the attractions of tea. It is, of course, possible that among his tribe of cats, there was one creature of bizarre tastes which was partial to the leaf. A wicked, but interesting Steinlen cat, jet-black and baleful of eye, announced the re-opening of the *Chat Noir* theatre restaurant in Paris, and a quartet of indulgent cats joined a beautiful woman and three dogs to advertise a veterinary clinic. In another famous poster, again for an art exhibition, a languorous tabby reclines hugely across the entire surface of the announcement, its paws deftly pointing to the essential message.

Peugeot chooses the biggest cat to promote the power and reliability of its cycles, early in this century. The poster shows the firm's Paris building. The value is around £100/$160.

Turning to the collector's domain of the three-dimensional cat, there is no more keenly sought commodity at the present time than the range of small 'cold-painted bronze' animals, most of which originated in Vienna between the 1880s and the 1920s. These delightful toy novelties measure from in height 5-10cm (2-4in) and were cast in a bronze alloy (some of the less expensive ones are lead-based), the models being painted later when the metal had cooled, usually as tabbies or greys. Although only infrequently dressed in clothes, the animals are nearly always engaged in human pursuits and are the nearest thing to a bronze incarnation of Louis Wain's feline sprites. Were they directly influenced by Wain's art? Was he influenced by the Viennese cats, which sold in novelty shops in Britain? Certainly the two genres of art were contemporary with each other, and the questions intrigue collectors.

Feline fever had been creeping over the collector market for a couple of decades from the mid-1960s, but its most virulent

Above: Art of the big cat. One of a set of five bone china plaques of African wildlife, after paintings by David Shepherd for the Boehm porcelain factory. In 1980 a set sold for £3,000/$4,800 and the value has been steadily increasing.

Below: A pair of Ralph Wood ceramic models of lions, *c.*1700, on the ball at more than £5,000/$8,000 in the late 1980s.

bout, the Viennese strain, can be traced to the mid 1980s when a remarkable collection of these little cats came on the market *en masse*. There were about 250 of them which had belonged to a British collector whose grandfather bought them mainly in Austria and Germany between 1900 and 1920 when they cost a few shillings per piece or even per group. Anna Marrett, head of the department of dolls and related items at Phillips, had some misgivings — the appearance in the saleroom of such a large collection at one time might depress the market. But, in the event, her fears were dispelled when cat prices ran wild. The collection realized £25,000 or nearly $40,000.

In this collection, which was representative of the huge range of activities available, cats played croquet, served dinner, chopped wood, painted canvases, taught and chastized kittens, rode rocking horses and dogs, peered through telescopes, operated cameras, flew kites. There were cats in floppy chef hats, carrying the tools of their trade: one brandished a butter tub, one a copper pan, another a mixing bowl; they displayed joints of meat and a huge fish on platters; one wrestled with a struggling pig. Cats appeared playing musical instruments, joining in sport, gardening. Just about anything a human being can do, a Viennese bronze cat can do. Twelve-piece orchestras were the stars of this amazing menagerie. They reached up to £700/$1,120 in bids at the time, and since then some dealers reckon their prices have more than doubled.

Cold painted bronze cats from Austria (made between 1880 and 1920) beguile collectors. Units of up to a dozen musicians are reaching towards £1,000/$1,600 in value. Here are some of the bronze cats' antics.

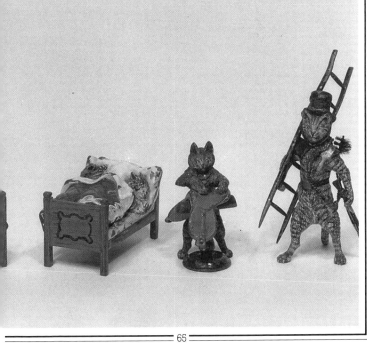

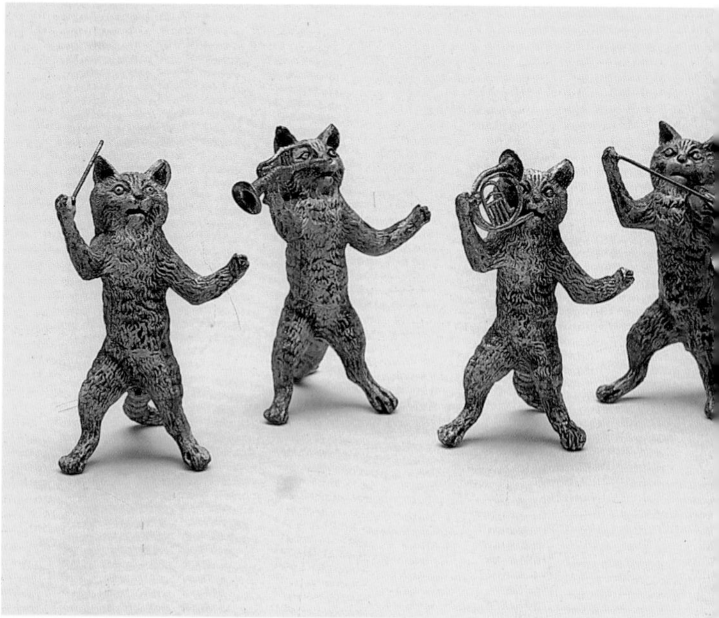

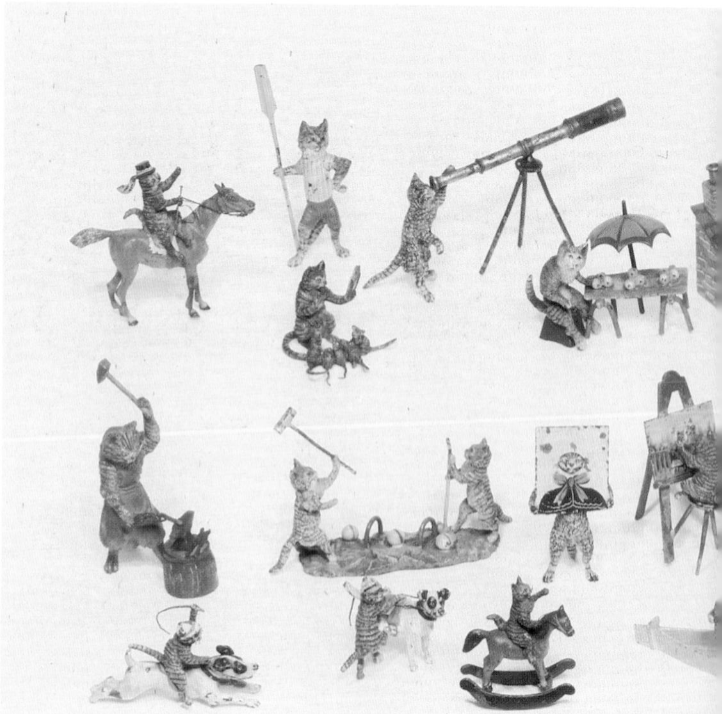

Left: These 8cm (3in) high musicians are from Vienna, made in cold painted bronze. They date from the early part of this century and would cost about £150-£200/$240-$320 in the late 1980s. (Author's collection).

Below: An extensive collection of the Viennese bronze cats, showing that their activities have a distinct Louis Wain flavour.

Below: Fabric and composition, a 'nodding head' tiger from the early twentieth century. He was the forerunner of dogs and cats who nodded through the 1960s rear windows of motor cars; £100-£150/$160-$240.

Bottom: William Henry Hamilton Trood was renowned for his dogs, but cats were winners too when he painted them. 'Women's Rights — A Meeting' is signed and dated 1885 (Bonhams, £3,000/$4,800).

Many cat collectors were unaware of, or little informed about, the existence of this breed of Viennese cats before the appearance of the definitive collection. Within the space of two years, however, the genre had become an important collecting theme, with more bronze cats appearing out of the attic as interest spread. Perhaps there are other kinds of treasures, yet 'undiscovered', to delight cat enthusiasts.

Writing in *The Times* in March 1988, Barbara Amiel observed, as a person 'devoted to dogs': 'Essentially, I think cats are psychopaths who have no sense of right or wrong, only a sense of desire or avoidance. They have no conscience. Cats love sardines and hate being kicked just as dogs adore liverwurst and loathe being bashed on the head. But while a judicious mixture of the two will make a dog perform marvels, cats, being psychopaths don't associate their own actions with the rewards or punishments that follow. They do whatever happens to please them at the moment, and view both sardines and kicks as unrelated chance occurences apportioned out by a deity as capricious as they are. ...Dogs crouch guiltily under a table when they have done something wrong. Cats may have eaten the entire goldfish population in the children's room, but if the goldfish tasted good, how could it be wrong to eat them? They can do no wrong and have nothing to feel guilty about, which is the definition of a psychopath...'

Psychopaths? Is this a case of libel? Cat lovers unite! Save up to buy yourself some feline jollity from Vienna — and renew your faith in cats.

Chapter Eight

STAR DOGS

Pluto came on the scene in 1930, although he was not named as such until 1931, and today, in comfortable middle age, he is still being collected. In collectors' hoards there are undeniably, more images of Pluto than any other dog the world ever knew. Among Disney collectables he doesn't match the popularity of his master, Mickey Mouse, nor that of Donald Duck, but he is treasured in a multitude of artefacts, ranging through wrist-watches, towels, marionettes, pyjama cases, ashtrays, calendars, paint-boxes, egg-cups, lamps, toys of every description and just about every other thing that was made with the Disney name on it.

Pluto memorabilia from the 1930s is the main target of the dedicated collectors. Because of its rarity and its cost, however, many people have now moved to the Fifties era as a hunting ground. Postwar Marx toys and those of a score of other makers are clattering to success on their sturdy clockwork motors.

Collectors of Pluto have to know the background of the early Disney cartoons. A rubber Pluto, 10cm (4in) high and 17cm (7in) long, made in 1934 by Sieberling Latex Products of Akron, Ohio, is found in a startling red colour, with black and white features picked out. A *red* Pluto? Can it be

right? It is very much right. Pluto's colour was irrelevant in those early years when the cartoon films were black and white. His now familiar yellow-ochre hue was not established until 1937-38, after which all films featuring Mickey and Pluto were in colour.

Pluto comes in many forms — 'hunting' with Mickey, riding a rail trolley-car with Donald, coupled with that other famous Disney dog, Goofy, or on his own as a wind-up novelty, a marionette (between 1933 and 1939 Macy's and other big US stores marketed Pluto puppets by the thousand), or a velvet covered doll. In the late Thirties the Knickerbocker Toy Company of New York issued Mickey, Donald, Pluto and Goofy dolls in velvet or a fabric called duvetyne, advertised as 'cuddle or stand-up models'. Pluto stood at 40cm (16in) and, like the rest, was designed by Charlotte Clark. The Lionel Corporation of New York sold the Donald Duck railcar for $1.25 in 1936; Donald commands at the rear and Pluto sticks out his black-bobbed snout at the front. Today, it is heading towards $2,000/£1,250 at Disney auctions in America, when in mint condition and contained in its original box.

Robert Lesser, a Disney collector whose New York apartment is crammed from ceiling to floor with juvenilia,

Everybody knows him. Here, Pluto makes an appearance as a pottery figure from Japan. Pluto figures vary enormously in value from £30/$48 to many hundreds, depending on age, medium and rarity.

places high store by Pluto, of whom he has many examples in various media. Pluto and other Disney characters were made in quantity by European manufacturers before the Second World War and this catchment area fascinates Lesser. He maintains: 'If collectors could go through every foreign newspaper of the 1930s, published in the weeks leading up to Christmas, they would discover advertisements for many, many toys in print that have never actually been found.' He likes to think that so many Mickey Mouse objects were made throughout the world at the start of the Thirties because 'Mickey was eternally optimistic and optimism helped to make this creature the best salesman of the Depression era'. Pluto, Mickey's best friend, dog-extraordinary, rightly shares in that eminence.

Yes, Goofy is a dog. Here he is in a tinny duet with Donald Duck (Donald drums, Goofy dances), by Marx toys; £250-£350/$400-$560.

Snoopy dog seems set to make the running among the antiques of tomorrow collectables range from the widely available cuddly toys, in many sizes, to the exclusivity of an original drawing by the artist. Thurber dogs, on a smaller scale, have trod the path before Snoopy. Some dogs have carved or re-entered, their niche in history, simply *because* they have interested collectors. Few people, it could be argued, took much notice of Lord Byron's dogs until news neadlines in 1987 recorded the fact that a dog collar which belonged to one of them had made £2 100/$3,360 at auction.

Collars can be special, it seems. The annual Bonhams sale of dog memorabilia in London has also seen these items: a silver-studded collar engraved, 'I am Bob, Mrs King's dog, take me back to 1 Sloane Gardens, London SW'; a sixteenth century iron dog collar composed of multiple iron

Pluto again, this time under the direction of
Donald Duck aboard a Lionel rail car of 1936, now
worth considerably more than £1,000/$1,600 with
original box.

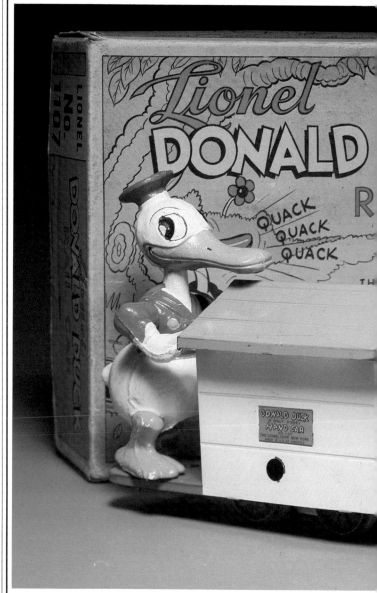

links with spikes, designed to protect the wearer when bear or wolf hunting; a leather collar studded with brass and engraved, 'New Jersey State Police'. Silver decoration and an interesting inscription increase the value — Bob's collar was priced at nearly £400/$640 in 1988; a simple beaded collar marked with the name of Sonny Boy, Barker, or Blackie, might be around the £50/$80 mark. (Fine art, of course is an important area where an inscription is valued. Sir Edwin Landseer signed an engraving of a Pomeranian and the work is inscribed with the words, 'To Mrs Eatwell in recollection of the Kindness in sending me the Spaniel puppy'). Bidders show their allegiance at dog sales; sample report in the *Antiques Trade Gazette*: 'One American couple in the saleroom displayed their particular fondness for Scotties, the wife decked out in Scottie jewellery and her husband with a Scottie tiepin'.

'Cat and dog pictures, illustrated books, postcards, bronzes, porcelain and pottery sell like mad,' says a Phillips auctioneer. 'Put "cat" or "dog" in a catalogue description and you just know that the lot is going to bring in the bids.' A bronze figure of a hound designed as an inkstand with the inkwell concealed beneath the hound's hinged head will reach £200/$320 at auction, a price enhanced by its canine character; there is a similar premium on items with a sporting flavour, golf, cricket or tennis. Dog bronzes are popular, so too are twentieth century enamel brooches which depict animals in comic poses or as straight portraits of different breeds. Highly desirable are small silver pin-cushions from the early part of this century, the main 'working' part being carried on the back of a fierce looking pug, a miniaturized St Bernard, or a bulldog. From the same period, the greyhound is a favourite choice for walking-stick heads in ivory.

It seems a fitting footnote to this chapter that Phillips, the auction house, the font of so many canine collectables, should owe a particular debt of gratitude to one dog, Friend. He was, indeed, the

Plus solide
que l'Acier
HUTCHINSON
d'après
Mich
PNEU VÉLO
HUTCHINSON
AFFICHES GAILLARD. PARIS. AMIENS

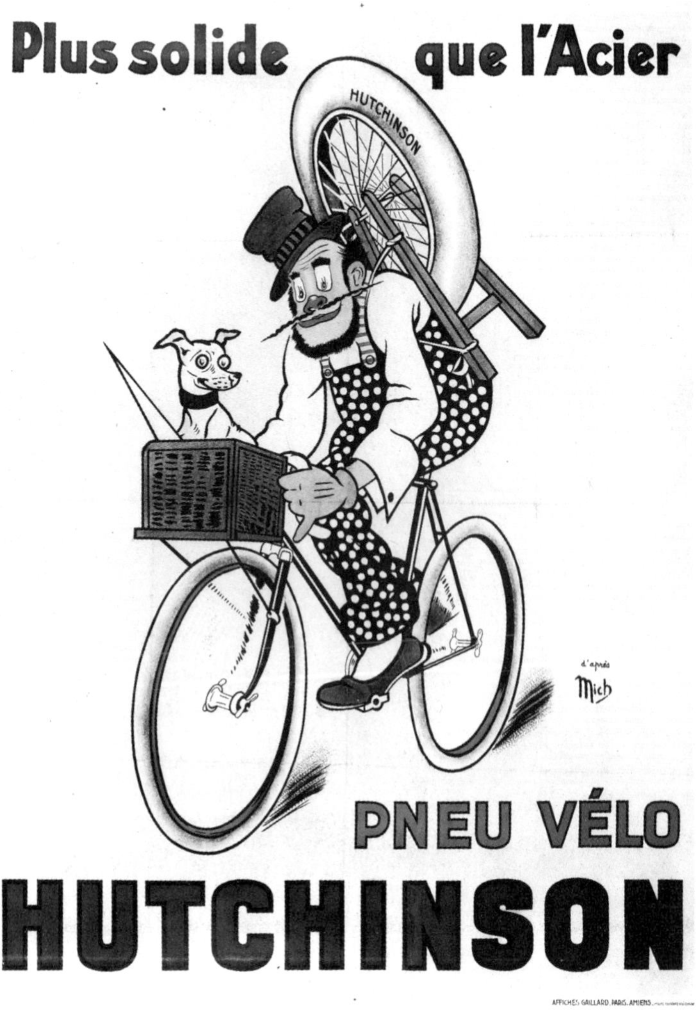

Dogs in French poster art. Bicycle posters from the first three decades of this century sell for around £100-£150/$160-$240 apiece.

best of friends to his master, Harry Phillips, the auctioneer who founded the firm in 1796 and built its fortunes during the exciting years of the early nineteenth century. The dog saved his life in circumstances that have left posterity an interesting legacy of collectables. An oil painting hanging in the entrance hall of the London salerooms shows a juvenile Harry, wearing ruff collar, posing with his dog by the

shore of a choppy sea; it bears a plaque, reading: 'Mr Phillips' dog Friend, reputed to have saved his life when in danger of drowning.'

Records are imprecise, but it appears that the youthful Harry was rescued by his dog from the waters of Portsmouth harbour; one account suggests the year was 1789, but this date is believed to be too late in time. However, apart from the oil painting, there are several objects of art which commemorate the event. A print after a painting by George Morland records the life-saving, and the scene has been discovered on a number of three-dimensional artefacts. One is a Victorian *papier-mâché* lap desk, or writing box, manufactured by McCallum & Hodson, of Birmingham, specialists in *papier-mâché*. These were not simply 'one-off' items — examples crop up from time to time, the affair having been something of a popular sensation in its day and one which

Right Royal Doulton character-model collectors know this fellow as 'Fox in Red Frock Coat'. He measures 16.5cm (6½in) in height, dates from 1938 and is capable of attracting bids of several hundred pounds or dollars.

Below: Small lead figures, not as expensive as the Viennese bronze models of cats, but an attractive collectors' item. Each dog has his day at about £20/$32. (Author's collection)

continued to be commemorated in early Victorian times. The canine hero was frequently portrayed on other objects of *papier-mâché* and in Staffordshire china figures. There seems to be some confusion over Friend's breed — some portraits suggest a collie, others have overtones of cocker spaniel — but he is generally shown bedraggled on a life raft. All accounts agree, however, that there would have been no Phillips without him: the dog is truly an auctioneer's best Friend.

Chapter Nine

ADVICE FOR
COLLECTORS

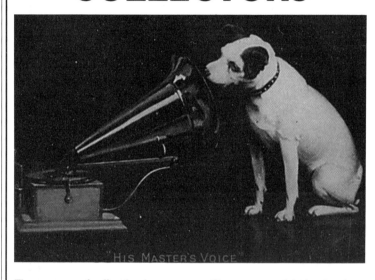

"HIS MASTER'S VOICE"

The essence of collecting is specialization. This view must be qualified, however, when it is applied to collections of memorabilia relating to cats and dogs. An enthusiast might have a perfectly valid collection which is made up of works of art and artefacts of many types and media — pictures, ceramics, ephemera, books and toys, to list but a few. There lies the attraction of a subject such as cats and dogs: it covers a field that can appeal to eclectic tastes. Within the very wide boundaries, however, the disciplines of specialization may be followed if the collector so wishes.

One avenue might be the dog paintings of Sir Edwin Landseer (if the pocket runs to it), and the school of or works after the artist. A collector may wish to go for the lighter vein of William Henry Hamilton Trood, or dog pictures by modern painters. Similarly, Louis Wain presents a specialization opportunity that offers much choice. His postcards are an obvious, and relatively inexpensive, area; there are also his books, or even his original watercolours, all sufficiently available in numbers to give scope for specialization. The cats of the early potters, the works of Derby, Rockingham or Whieldon,

Left: His fame went round the world with the music he listened to, His Master's Voice dog, seen here on a pre-war postcard.

Below: Attributed to Lucy Walker: 'Kennel Mates', typical of the Victorian genre of painting dogs; dated 1878; value is around £1,000/$1,600.

the Viennese bronzes and similar models, cat figures in lead and tin, or cartoon cats and dogs; the roll is considerable.

Whatever character the collection assumes, the basic principles remain. The collector should always buy the best that he or she can afford, be extremely discriminating, and aim for items in perfect condition, remembering that damaged objects may cost heavily to repair and almost certainly will be difficult to 'move' by trading in or reselling. Collections can be refined as time passes and the acquisition of knowledge and experience leads to more

Right: Dog bronzes such as this small example marked P.J. Mene have been steadily rising in value.

Below: A circus dog stars in a cigarette card — one of a set of Clowns issued by Taddy's at the turn of the century. It has become the most expensive set of cigarette cards, having made a sensational £17,000/$27,200 at a Phillips auction.

Left: Cat style exemplified in an etching, the work of Tsuguharu Foujita, 'Sitting Cat'; £500-£800/ $800-$1,280.

Below: Bonzo, a plated metal mascot which might have graced the radiator cap of a motor car in the period before the 1939-1945 war; £50-£100/$80-$160.

A Victorian metal novelty consisting of a
clockwork dog-fight with mechanical sound.

discriminating taste.

Robert Lesser, a New York
collector of Disneyana, has some
shrewd comments to make about
collectors generally (quoted in
*Walt Disney's Mickey Mouse
Memorabilia*, Octopus Books,
London, 1986). He describes two
major categories of collector:
long-distance runners and
short-distance 'sweaters', and
considers himself one of the
former. The passion of the
short-distance collector is
intense, but burns itself out in six
months. When the burn-out
comes, the short-distance
collector sells up. The long-
distance collector goes on
because he recognizes and
appreciates the real values of
artistry or craftsmanship in the
objects which he collects.
Between the two groups of
collectors, there are those who
only want to buy cheaply and are
so price-conscious that they build
up vast collections of 'garbage'.
And there are a rare few who
assemble a relatively small
collection of superb pieces, the
whole honed to perfection by
discriminating decisions.

Gottfried Mind, who lived and worked in Bern, Switzerland, was known as the Raphael of Cats. This fine print of 1820, after one of his works, shows the delicacy of his line.

Mel Birnkrant, of Massachusetts, a fellow collector, is more impressed by a small collection that has a few outstanding pieces than by a huge hoard that contains nothing he would like to find for himself. He is on record in the *Mickey Mouse* book as saying: 'Fate dictates what you are going to get. Other collectors are going to get something that you are never going to have, and each collection, whatever its size, has its own character.'

Left: A set of English late nineteenth-century ninepin dogs made of stuffed felt and with wooden bases. The kingpin wears a scarlet coat and a braided crown; 20cm (8in) high, £200-£300/$320-$480.

Below left: Canine painters often grouped two dogs of different breeds for effect — as in 'Watchers', an 1885 painting by Briton Riviere.

Learn the basic look, 'feel' and very nature of your subject matter by browsing at antique fairs, trawling the antique dealers' shops and attending auction views. Seek the advice of reputable dealers and auction room staff; it is freely given by both. If you are planning to bid at a saleroom and you are new to the experience, monitor the pace and prices at a few auctions before taking the plunge; and *always* read the catalogue carefully. Some dealers have begun to specialize in cat and dog subject matter. Auction houses are now giving the themes more attention than hitherto. General collectors' sales, which often include toys and novelties, can be a rewarding hunting ground. On the other hand, animal subjects are among the high-flyers at some of the most prestigious picture sales. The fine art of collecting cats and dogs has a bright and exciting future.

Left: Messrs Cat, Poodle and Fox, from a range of Cococubs supplied by Britain's, the toy-soldier maker, to Cadbury's for inclusion in cocoa packets during the inter-war years. Figures average a few pounds apiece. (Author's collection)

Far left below: He is a contender for the title of the world's most famous cartoon cat: Felix, who kept on walking into collectors' hearts long after his cinema days were over. Here he appears in various forms.

Below: A pair of Victorian papier-mâché hand fans, painted with dog subjects, at Bonhams. One can be seen on page 88 and the other is entitled 'A distinguished member of the humane society', and appears to be yet another rendering of Friend, the dog that saved the life of the youthful Harry Phillips, founder of Phillips auction house. Compare it with the colour picture of a papier-mâché table on page 22.

Acknowledgements

The author's thanks go to the staff of Phillips, specialists in many departments whose daily duties bring them into contact with the images of cats and dogs in art, antiques and collectors' items; and to Christopher Halton, Diana Kay and Jacqueline Barber for their help in providing Phillips illustrations. Among many other sources, I have borrowed the words or thoughts of Christopher Forbes, Henry Sandon and C. Eileen King. The great majority of photographs were supplied by Phillips. In addition, a special debt of gratitude is owed to Isobel Glenny of Bonhams for her kind and fulsome assistance and to the company for permission to publish certain illustrations from sales held to coincide with the annual Crufts show in London. Finally, the author remembers Susy and Splashdown, who in the happy past have snoozed in his study through many an hour of word-creation, and to whom this book is affectionately dedicated.